TRIUMPH
ENTERTAINMENT

• Contents •

Inside this Book

Credits

Editor in Chief: Bill Gill, a.k.a. "Pojo"

Creative Director & Graphic Design:
Jon Anderson, a.k.a. "JonnyO"

Project Manager: Bob Baker

Contributors:

Jae Kim, Justin Webb, Matthew J.
Murphy, Jason Cohen, Alex Searcy,
Alex Butschli, Karl Povey,
Ken Hartwick, Michael Lucas, Dan
Peck, Joseph Lee, Mike Rosenberg,
Chris Snapp, Bryan Camareno, and
Amy Gill.

It's time to start training harder!

The Yu-Gi-Oh! cartoon (anime) sets some great examples for those of you who want to become expert duelists.

Trading cards with your friends can make all your decks better.

Training with your friends will help you understand how cards work, and help you fine-tune your decks.

I asked a lot of my friends to help me write this book. Some of them are among the top players in World. They have a lot of cool Yu-Gi-Oh! secrets to share with you to help you become a better duelist.

Enjoy!

Pojo

The Top Fifty Cards You Should Be Playing!

By: Jae Kim (a.k.a. JAELOVE)

1. Pot of Greed

Legend of Blue Eyes - LOB-119

This card is number one. Every player should use Pot of Greed because it gives you two cards for the price of one! Having more

cards than your opponent in a duel is always a good thing, so pack a Pot of Greed in every deck.

2. Graceful Charity

Starter Deck Pegasus - SDP-040

Isn't it cool how the two best cards in the game cost only a dollar each? You should put Graceful Charity in your deck because it gives you more cards, and it lets you keep the better ones. Keeping the three best cards and throwing away the two worst seems like a good idea.

Do you have these cards in your deck?

GRACEFUL CHARITY
[MAGIC CARD]

SDP-040

Draw 3 cards from your Deck, then discard any 2 cards from your hand.

©1996 KAZUKI TAKAHASHI

79571449

3. Delinquent Duo

Magic Ruler - MRL-039

Delinquent Duo may be an old card but it's also very good. One thousand life points seems like a lot to pay, but you'll be able to take away two of your opponent's cards for only one of yours! You will have more options than him, making a win easier.

4. Breaker the Magical Warrior

Magician's Force - MFC-071

Everybody loves Breaker. He can destroy a spell or trap and has 1900 attack. You should play him. Try to trade for one or buy it if you must. It's a very good card that should go in every deck.

5. Sangan

Metal Raiders - MRD-069

Sangan should read as "Find any monster with 1500 or less attack and use it instead of this card." Even if something destroys it, you still get to use it. Sangan is a great card at any points during a duel.

6. Heavy Storm

Metal Raiders - MRD-142

Heavy Storm is the only card in the game that gets rid of every one of your opponent's spell/trap cards at the same time. If you want to attack, you'll need this card.

7. Black Luster Soldier· Envoy of the Beginning

Invasion of Chaos - IOC-025

Everyone thinks Black Luster Soldier-Envoy of the Beginning is awesome, and for good reason. Once he hits the field, BLS is the most powerful monster card in the game. Try to trade for it if you can, because it's one of the best monsters in the game.

8. Sinister Serpent

Video Game Promo - SDD-002

This card might look weak, but it keeps coming back to your hand. It is very annoying, since you can keep setting it to draw your opponent's monsters out. It also works well with Graceful Charity and other combo cards.

9. Ring of Destruction

Pharaonic Guardian - PGD-001

Because this card can chain to your opponent's spell/trap removal, it's the best Trap card in the game. You can destroy anything and do life point damage as well! It is very helpful.

10. Call of the Haunted

Pharaoh's Servant - PSV-012

Being able to bring more of your own monsters on to the field is a good bet. Call of the Haunted is the best way to do so. Even if you use it on a Jinzo or a Sangan, they destroy it, you'll get the effect!

11. Mystical Space Typhoon

Magic Ruler - MRL-047

Mystical Space Typhoon is the second best spell/trap remover in the game. It's Spell Speed 2, so it can chain to anything. This is a good way to disturb your opponent's strategy. It should go into any deck that wants to attack.

12. Snatch Steal

Magic Ruler - MRL-036

Snatch Steal lets you steal one of your opponent's monsters for a bit. Just be careful; if you take a monster and can't do any life point damage, your opponent will gain lots of life points.

13. Mirror Force

Metal Raiders - MRD-138

This is the most feared card in the game because it can knockout 3-4 monsters at one time. It's a very good defensive card. It makes sense to include Mirror Force.

14. Spirit Reaper

Pharaonic Guardian - PGD-076

Spirit Reaper is very annoying. It acts like a defensive wall. This means your opponent must target it, in order to destroy it. It is hard to get rid of this card. Also, if it attacks and it works, it will discard your opponent's resource as well

15. Tribe-Infecting Virus

Magician's Force - MFC-076

Tribe-Infecting Virus mixes a good 1600 attack score with one of the best effects in the game. You can wipe out your opponent's entire field with this bad boy.

16. Ceasefire

Pharaoh's Servant - PSV-030

Ceasefire isn't given enough credit by many duelists. It can do a number of things, including life point damage, stopping flip effects, and protecting your own monsters from Nobleman of Crossout.

17. Premature Burial

Pharaoh's Servant - PSV-037

Premature Burial is a lot like Call of the Haunted, except you have to pay 800 life points and it works instantly (instead of having to set it and wait). Unfortunately, it can't chain, so it's ranked a wee bit lower.

18. D.D. Assailant

Video Game Promo - DBT-EN002

D.D Assailant will take the place of D.D Warrior Lady in many decks. It has a high attack score and will get rid of anything that strikes it. Sounds good, doesn't it?

9

19. Torrential Tribute

Labyrinth of Nightmare - LON-025
Torrential Tribute is the first card from Labyrinth of Nightmare to make the list. Oh what a good card it is! It will let you wipe out the entire field, making it a very scary card for your opponent.

20. Nobleman of Crossout

Pharaoh's Servant - PSV-034
Nobleman of Crossout changed the game when it came out. Before its release, cards like Man-Eater Bug were all over the place. Now, your opponent needs to be more careful with his flip monsters.

21. D.D. Warrior Lady

Dark Crisis - DCR-027
Everybody loves D.D. Warrior Lady. It's a Light monster with a solid effect. You are only allowed one in your deck, so you have no reason not to use it. Go get one!

22. Jinzo

Pharaoh's Servant - PSV-000
Jinzo is used by almost everyone who owns one. He will stop your opponent's traps. This effect is powerful. It can swing things in your favor.

23. Scapegoat

Starter Deck Joey - SDJ-041

Everyone's favorite sheep tokens do a number of things once they hit the field. They work defensively, but also combo with Metamorphosis, Enemy Controller, Creature Swap in very powerful ways.

24. Magician of Faith

Metal Raiders - MRD-036

Because Change of Heart is banned, it makes Magician of Faith easy to use. You can run her in two's and three's to get back the good spell cards. Watch out for Nobleman of Crossout.

25. Lightning Vortex

Flaming Eternity - FET-EN040

This new card from Flaming Eternity has the power to get rid of every single one of your opponent's monsters. It is one of the best cards in the game, although not as great as some people might believe.

26. Blade Knight

Collector Tin Set - CT1-EN002

Blade Knight is one of the few Light monsters that can actually use good attack. It also stops pesky flip effect monsters.

27. Slate Warrior

Video Game Promo - WC4-003
Slate Warrior is the best Flip effect monster and Fiend in the game. It's the best Flip because it can attack. If you want to run Night Assailant, you'll want to use this card too. It's a Fiend with a solid attack and two decent effects.

28. Berserk Gorilla

Invasion of Chaos - IOC-013
Berserk Gorilla is a simple but effective beatdown tool. You can put him into any deck, but he especially shines in Earth Beatdown and Beast Decks.

29. Swords of Revealing Light

Legend of Blue Eyes - LOB-101
If you protect it, Swords is the best stalling card in the game. It'll buy you three free turns of protection. It will also turn face down monsters up, eliminating nasty surprises your opponent might have planned for you.

30. Airknight Parshath

Legacy of Darkness - LOD-062
This is the second best tribute monster in the game. Its extra draw power is nice. It is one of the Light type cards with trample. So it can break through your opponent's Scapegoat tokens.

31. Apprentice Magician

Magician's Force - MFC-066

Apprentice Magician is often forgotten and not considered a top card. However, it finds Magician of Faith for you, and works as a Dark monster. It also can find Magical Scientist, Hand of Nepththys, and Old Vindictive Magician, not to mention Time Wizard.

32. Sacred Phoenix of Nephthys

Flaming Eternity - FET-EN005

This is the second best card out of Flaming Eternity. It is the best two-tribute monster in the game. On the field, it is hard to destroy. Use it in a FIRE deck, or try to run Hands of Nephthys to get it out quicker.

33. Cyber Jar

Magic Ruler - MRL-077

Cyber Jar is the best "reset" now that Fiber Jar is gone. Using it will clear the field and provide a path for new monsters. Its luck factor is pretty high though, so be careful.

34. Sakuretsu Armor

Dark Crisis - DCR-102

This card is a mini-Mirror Force. If you want more monster removal mixed with defense, run this card. It hass lost a little since the return of Mirror Force, but it is still a very good trap card.

35. smashing Ground

Invasion of Chaos - IOC-093
Smashing Ground is the same as Sakuretsu Armor. While you lose defense, you can use it on cards like Spirit Reaper that might be stalling. It also works versus Jinzo. It's also ready to play right away.

36. Magic Drain

Pharaoh's Servant - PSV-071
With the return of Graceful Charity and Delinquent Duo, stopping spells is important once again. Magic Drain can help stop powerful spells from hurting your chances of winning.

37. Book of Moon

Pharaonic Guardian - PGD-035
This is the "Swiss-Army" knife of Yu-Gi-Oh! It works as defense, and offense, It helps you re-use flip effects, it combos with all sorts of cards, and it prevents your opponent's traps and spells. It's also very good in a side deck.

38. united we stand

Labyrinth of Nightmare - LON-049
This is the best equip card in the game. Using it with a card like Scapegoat means a monstrous 4000 attack bonus. It can do quite well, but your mileage may vary.

39. Zombrya the Dark

Labyrinth of Nightmare - LON-074
Zombrya is a rare Dark Warrior type. It can knockout Berserk Gorilla, Dark Balter, Airknight Parshath, basically making it a powerful field presence. Because it is searchable by Reinforcement of the Army, Zombrya the Dark is highly recommended for any deck that needs Dark monsters.

40. Magic Cylinder

Labyrinth of Nightmare - LON-104
Magic Cylinder doesn't create card advantage. However, it can be the scariest card in the game for your opponent if he is low on life points. Magic Cylinder has the power to end games. It should go into decks that deal life point damage quickly.

41. Injection Fairy Lily

Legacy of Darkness - LOD-100
Injection Fairy Lily is the most powerful summonable monster in the game, with an impressive 3400 attack. Of course, you'll have to pay 2000 life points each time you use her effect, so be careful.

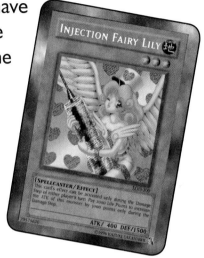

42. Morphing Jar

Tournament Pack Season 2 - TP2-001
Morphing Jar is an expensive card, but it is worth it for decks that need that extra draw power. The downside is that your opponent gets five cards too. This is another card that requires good luck to use well.

43. Card Destruction

Starter Deck Yugi - SDY-O42
Card Destruction is for decks that need extra draw power. In these decks, it's super valuable, although it requires good luck at times.

45. Windstorm of Etaqua

Video Game Promo - PCY-OO1
Windstorm of Etaqua will slice up decks that rely on Scapegoat and Berserk Gorillas. It is a very good card, often better than Enemy Controller. It can lead to heavy card advantage when used correctly.

44. Mobius the Frost Monarch

Soul of Duelist - SOD-ENO22
Mobius the Frost Monarch is very good against decks that run non-chainable traps like Sakuretsu Armor, and also against Burn decks. It has good stats and a great effect. This makes it a solid monster.

46. Enemy Controller

Ancient Sanctuary - AST-O37
Enemy Controller is a solid card from Ancient Sanctuary that has two decent effects. Both effects aren't great on their own, but when combined you have a useful card.

47. Thunder Dragon

Metal Raiders - MRD-097

Thunder Dragon will work with Lightning Vortex, Card Destruction, Monster Reincarnation, Dark Core, Graceful Charity, and against Delinquent Duo, and many other cards. It's also an easy Light monster and great to use with Metamorphosis.

49. Dark Magician of Chaos

Invasion of Chaos - IOC-065

This is the second best two-tribute monster in the game. It is a Dark type, which helps it greatly; getting any spell card that you want from the graveyard, coupled with a 2800 attack, makes it a heavy hitter. Keep in mind it's difficult to get onto the field.

48. Metamorphosis

Pharaonic Guardian - PGD-090

Metamorphosis combos very well with Sinister Serpent, Magician of Faith/ Apprentice Magician, Scapegoat, and other such cards. It can be unstable, but if you run a lot of the cards mentioned, Metamorphosis has a very powerful effect. It can help win a few duels.

50. Blowback Dragon

Ancient Sanctuary - AST-022

The final card on our list is the nifty Blowback Dragon, a card that packs 2300 attack, DARK status, and a very powerful effect. If you get the coin flip right and you can destroy any card in the game!

How to talk like a Pro
A Yu-Gi-Oh! CCG Dictionary

By: Ace of spades

As a duelist, there are some **"sayings"** you should understand. They're easy to remember and make you seem smarter in the process!

Metagame – describes common themes, trends and ideas in the local area where you play.

> *Example: "Spear Dragon is popular in the metagame now."*

Top-Decking – when you have no cards in your hand and continue to draw.

> *Example: "I top-decked an Exiled Force and destroyed his Jinzo."*

Side Deck – when you take a card from your main deck and put it back into your side deck.

> *Example: "My opponent side-decked his Magic Cylinder for a Ring of Destruction."*

Main Deck – when you take a card from your side deck and put it into the main deck.

> *Example: "I main-decked my Kinetic Soldier to counter his warriors."*

Sanctioned Tournament – Tournaments that have been approved by Upper Deck Entertainment.

> *Example: "I came in third at a sanctioned tournament and won some cool prize cards."*

OTK – One-Turn Knockout; a combination of cards that can win the game in one turn

> Example: "I used the Yatagarasu to get an OTK."

FTK – First-Turn Knockout; a combination of cards that can win the game on the first turn

> Example: "I drew Megamorph, Cyber-Stein, Raigeki and Harpie's Feather Duster in my first hand and got an FTK."

Yata-Lock – when you cannot draw due to the opponent's use of Yatagarasu

Beatstick – monster with 1800 or higher ATK with 4 stars, for example, Kycoo, Berserk Gorilla

Cookie-Cutter Deck – A good deck that is copied "card for card" by many players. An unoriginal deck, but usually a pretty good one.

> Example: "He's playing a Cookie Cutter Warrior deck."

At your next tournament, you'll be sounding just like a pro by using these simple phrases and shorthand! Other players will be amazed!

Common Yu-gi-oh! Abbreviations:

MST = Mystical Space Typhoon

BEWD = Blue Eyes White Dragon

REBD = Red Eyes Black Dragon

Ring/RoD = Ring of Destruction

Call/CotH = Call of the Haunted

CoH = Change of Heart

CED = Chaos Emperor Dragon

CED = Compulsory Evacuation Device

TT = Torrential Tribute

PoG/Pot = Pot of Greed

BLS-EotB = Black Luster Soldier – Envoy of the Beginning

BEUD = Blue Eyes Ultimate Dragon

V-Lord = Vampire Lord

TIV/T-Virus = Tribe Infecting Virus

X-force = Exiled Force

MoF = Magician of Faith

NoC = Nobleman of Crossout

SoRW = Swords of Revealing Light

GAF = Goblin Attack Force

What's HOT!
What's NOT!
A Quick Guide to What the Pros Use

By: Bryan Camareno

Hey everyone! I'm here to tell you what's hot and what's not hot this season in Yu-Gi-Oh! I'll tell you what tournaments to go to, what cards you should play, and what decks you should be playing.

Individual Cards

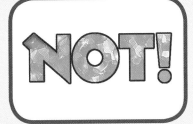

HOT!

- D.D. Assailant
- Sacred Phoenix of Nephthys
- Apprentice Magician
- Black Luster Soldier – Envoy of the Beginning
- Blade Knight
- Vampire Lord
- Dark Magician of Chaos
- Airknight Parshath
- Jinzo
- Scapegoat
- Berserk Gorilla
- King Tiger Wanghu
- Enraged Battle Ox
- Enemy Controller
- Book of Moon
- Mirror Force
- Torrential Tribute
- Delinquent Duo
- Magician of Faith
- Breaker the Magical Warrior
- Graceful Charity
- Lightning Vortex
- Nobleman of Crossout
- Smashing Ground
- Mobius the Frost Monarch
- Pyramid Turtle
- Creature Swap

NOT!

- Gradmarg the Earth Monarch
- Thestalos the Firestorm Monarch
- Zaborg the Thunder Monarch
- Mystic Tomato
- Giant Rat
- Mother Grizzly
- Spear Dragon
- Peten the Dark Clown
- Blue-Eyes White Dragon
- Red-Eyes Black Dragon
- Red-Eyes Darkness Dragon
- Vampire Genesis
- Mind Control
- Chiron the Mage
- Kaiba Man
- Dark Magician
- Harpies
- Monster Reincarnation
- The Creator
- Archfiend of Gilfer
- Luminous Soldier
- Magical Thorn
- Soul Exchange

Check the Yu-Gi-Oh! Card of the Day section at www.pojo.com for more details on what cards to use or not use.

Card Sets

- Flaming Eternity
- Invasion of Chaos
- Dark Crisis
- Legacy of Darkness
- Pharaonic Guardian
- Dark Beginnings 1
- Dark Revelations

- Rise of Destiny
- Soul of the Duelist
- Ancient Sanctuary

Tournaments

- Shonen Jump Championships
- Yu-Gi-Oh! Nationals 2005
- Regional Tournaments
- Official Local Tournaments

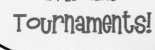

Me like Tournaments!

Formats

- Advanced Format with the April 1st Ban List.
- Yu-Gi-Oh! Sealed Pack and Draft

- Traditional Format (Without the April 1st, 2005 Ban List)

Decks

- Chaos/Warrior
- Chaos/Zombie
- Chaos/Control
- Chaos
- Chaos/Phoenix
- Phoenix/Zombie
- Warriors
- Zombies
- Zombie/Control
- Earth Beat-down
- Beast-down
- Deck-Out
- Control
- Silent Swordsman
- Beat-down
- Gravekeepers

- Horus
- Armed Dragon
- Burn/Stall
- Dark Magician
- Mystic Swordsman
- Water/Stall
- Water Beat-down
- Beasts

A Beginner's Guide to Yu-Gi-Oh!

By: SiphonX

Every Duelist begins by reading the Yu-Gi-Oh! rule book that comes with every starter deck.

If you're just starting out in the world of Yu-Gi-Oh!, you're not alone. Many people have just begun and are wondering exactly what to put in their deck. Putting cards in your deck that don't fit with each other can be a bad mistake.

The deck should start out with a **"theme,"** or idea from which to build upon. This may seem hard, but it is not. The theme is just the idea of the cards you put in your deck. These themes range from Monster Types like Warriors and Dragons to Attributes like Darks, but they do not stop there. By using a **central idea**, a player is able to put in cards that fit that theme. Once you select your theme, you can start making the deck itself.

Start by using cards that would be in your theme. If you decide to play Warriors, a good place to start is a strong Warrior base, with cards like Marauding Captain, Goblin Attack Force, Reinforcement of the Army and Mataza the Zapper.

If you don't have much money, do not worry about the cost of the cards. Instead, use cheaper substitutes and save money for the cards you want. By remembering that your deck must have **at least forty cards,** you need to build a strong Monster base as well as **Spells** and **Traps.**

One needs to have a deck that has enough Monster destruction, or Spells and Traps that destroy Monsters. Smashing Ground and Sakuretsu Armor are good and cheap choices. These cards will help you clear the field for attacking. Also, supportive Spells and Traps that help your Monsters are good as well, like Snatch Steal (see page 8), Swords of Revealing Light (see page 12), Scapegoat (see page 11), and Book of Moon (see page 14).

A side DECK contains 15 cards of your choice.

Finally, there are cards that are must haves for a good deck. These cards usually have effects so good that it would be a mistake not to include them. These include: **Pot of Greed** (see page 4), **Premature Burial** (see page 9), **Heavy Storm** (see page 6), **Change of Heart, Call of the Haunted** (see page 7), **Tribe-Infecting Virus** (see page 9), **Breaker the Magical Warrior** (see page 6), **and Sinister Serpent** (see page 7). There are many more, and they are expensive. These are the cards you want to save your money for.

If you follow these tips, you should be able to make a good deck. Just remember not to get so caught up in the competition, but to have fun!

Simple Tips to Building a Great Deck

Without Spending Much Money

By: Coin Flip

1. Cut out monsters with low ATK or DEF and no effect! Too many times I see a card like Baby Dragon or Dark Magician in a deck while better cards like **Man-Eater Bug** and **Insect Knight** are ignored. The stronger your monsters are (whether it's ATK or DEF), the more likely they won't be destroyed by your opponent's monsters. Insect Knight, Summoned Skull, Skilled Dark Magician and Mad Dog of Darkness are all very easy to get cards with strong ATK points! If you see any monsters with **2000 or more** DEF, they're good too. Prickle Fairy is really good because she has strong DEF and a good effect that will put your opponent's monsters in defense position, making them easier to knockout.

2. Good effects on monsters are a great thing! Man-Eater Bug and Night Assailant are weak, but they can destroy your opponent's monsters. You can take out your opponent's strongest monster in exchange! **Penguin Soldier** can flip two monsters back to the owner's hand, leaving your opponent open for attack!

3. Keep up with the **Banned and Restricted List** on the official web site! If you have cards on the list, but they aren't in your deck, there might be a chance you don't see some hidden uses for the cards. Try them out! You might like what you find.

4. Be Smart When You Buy Card Packs! If you don't have much money to spend on the game, **make it count!** Buy Dark Revelations packs or the new Structure decks. The Dragon's Roar Deck comes with 1 copy of a lot of powerful magic and trap cards, and the Zombie Madness Deck is just plain ridiculous – I won a tournament using it!

The Zoo A Beast Deck

By: snapper

Everyone loves animals. The Yu-Gi-Oh! Trading Card Game has a lot of animals. Let's try to mix the animal kingdom and Yu-Gi-Oh! together. Let's make a **Beast Deck,** and try to use easy to find cards.

- **Enraged Battle Ox** is not only a beast, but he also helps the rest of your Beasts on the field become even stronger. We'll use 3.

- Gorillas are one the smartest and strongest members of the animal kingdom. That's true in the game of Yu-Gi-Oh! too, so we'll use **3 Berserk Gorillas** (see page 12).

- You can't have a zoo without tigers, so we'll use **2 King Tiger Wanghus.** They should help keep the weaker monsters under control.

- Baboons are those creepy animals that everyone avoids. Yu-Gi-Oh! has an equal to these weird monkeys in the form of **Bazoo the Soul-Eater,** of which we'll use 2. For every defeated monster in your Graveyard. Bazoo can gain 300 ATK points.

- Squirrels will never be on exhibit in a zoo, but they do turn up in the eating areas. To honor the little fuzz balls, we'll use **3 Nimble Momongas.** When one dies in battle you can summon some new Nimble Momongas from your Deck AND you gain 1000 Life Points.

- **Chiron the Mage** is a half horse monster with an effect that allows him to destroy an opponent's Spell or Trap Card. Because he's so useful we'll use 2 of him.

- Elephants are one of the most popular animals at the zoo, and in Yu-Gi-Oh! **Big-Tusked Mammoth** rules the Beasts. While on the field, he scares all the opponent's monsters. With an ability like, that we have to use 2.

Toss in some standard Spells and Traps (most of which you can obtain by buying a Dragon's Roar Structure Deck), and you have a good and cheap Beast Deck.

A legal deck must contain at least 40 cards.

The Zoo A Beast Deck

Monsters:
2 – Big-Tusked Mammoth
3 – Enraged Battle Ox
3 – Berserk Gorilla
3 – Nimble Momonga
2 – King Tiger Wanghu
2 – Bazoo the Soul-Eater
2 – Chiron the Mage

Spells:
2 – Smashing Ground
2 – Nobleman of Crossout
2 – Swords of Concealing Light
2 – Scapegoat
2 – Creature Swap
1 – Pot of Greed
1 – Graceful Charity
1 – Heavy Storm
1 – Mystical Space Typhoon
1 – Snatch Steal
1 – Premature Burial

Traps:
2 – Sakuretsu Armor
2 – Dust Tornado
1 – Call of the Haunted
1 – Torrential Tribute
1 – Ceasefire

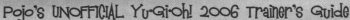

Your Best Friend, Your Rival

By: Dan Peck, aka Pook

Ever since the days of the first Pokèmon video game, my friend and I have always tried to be better than each other. Now, the same thing is true for Yu-Gi-Oh! Even though we are good friends, we still try to win, no matter what. Because of this, we've become even better duelists. You probably play Yu-Gi-Oh! against your friends more than any-one else. This means, you and your friends will duel with each other more than you will duel against other people at tournaments. Since you play against your friend or friends more, they are like your dueling rivals. This doesn't mean you aren't friends. No, think about it more like you are Yugi and your friend is Joey. In the cartoon, Yugi and Joey are best friends, but when it comes to dueling, they put that aside and try their best. The same thing happens with you! You know that beating your friend in a duel won't make him mad. Instead, he will be happy for you because you won and you are still best friends. This not only makes you a better duelist, but also better friends. Dueling brings people together.

Your rival may be your friend, your brother, your sister, even your mom or dad (if they play, of course).

He or she is there to test you, making you stronger and an even better player. Playing against your rival is a great way to practice for the big tournaments, because you don't have to worry about anything else. There is no pressure when you play your rival, except maybe a small bit that will help you win. But if you win, you aren't losing anything. All you are doing is making your friendship stronger.

I think it would be very good for all duelists to have a rival, so you can push yourself, making yourself stronger, both on the dueling field and off.

Happy dueling!

These two brothers get their game faces on for some fierce friendly family dueling!

How to Build Yugi's Deck

By: Alex Searcy a.k.a. Dark Paladin

ugi Moto is the favorite character of most people who watch the anime. We are going to teach you how to build a **Yugi deck**, and where to find the cards you need.

Most of these cards can be found in the **"Starter Evolution Deck: Yugi"**. The Starter Evolution Yugi deck sells for about $10.

You'll need some cards that won't be in the Evolution Starter. Here are the cards you'll need to trade for: Archfiend of Gilfer; Dark Magician Girl; Buster Blader; Alpha, Beta, Gamma, and Valkyrion the Magna Warriors; Breaker the Magical Warrior; Obnoxious Celtic Guardian; Big Shield Gardna; Polymerization; Diffusion; Wave-Motion; Graceful Charity; Exchange; Magic Cylinder; Mirror Force; and Time Seal.

Even though the cards are NOT found in the Evolution Starter deck, most can be found easily in other places.

Obnoxious Celtic Guardian and Buster Blader were released in a tin and Buster Blader was a Super Rare in Dark Beginnings. The Magnet Warriors are all Video Game promos.

Big Shield Gardna and Exchange are in Dark Beginnings also. Breaker can be found in Magician's Force. Magic Cylinder is an Invasion of Chaos special edition variant. Mirror Force can be found in Metal Raiders (which is a retired set so it may be hard to find.)

Although this deck may not be the best and may not win every duel, it is still pretty good, and a lot of fun to play.

Yugi's Deck List

Monsters x20
Tribute Monsters: x5
- **Dark Magician**
  (Learn more about using Dark Magician on page 52.)
- **Buster Blader**
- **Dark Magician Girl**
- **Summoned Skull**
- **Archfiend of Gilfer**

Non-Tribute x14
- **Alpha the Magnet Warrior**
- **Beta the Magnet Warrior**
- **Gamma the Magnet Warrior**
- **Valkyrion the Magnet Warrior**
- **Breaker the Magical Warrior**
- **Neo the Magic Swordsman**
- **Obnoxious Celtic Guardian**
- **Magician of Faith**
- **Gazelle the King of Mythical Beasts**
- **Sangan**
- **Big Shield Gardna**
- **Mystical Elf**
- **Giant Soldier of Stone**
- **Kuriboh**

Fusion:
- **Dark Paladin x1**
  (Goes in the Fusion deck)

Ritual:
- **Black Luster Soldier x1**

Spells x14:
- **Swords of Revealing Light**
- **Monster Reborn**
- **Change of Heart**
- **Mystical Space Typhoon**
- **Axe of Despair**
- **Pot of Greed**
- **Polymerization**
- **Card Destruction**
- **Black Luster Ritual**
- **Graceful Charity**
- **Diffusion Wave-Motion**
- **Dark Hole**
- **Mystic Plasma Zone**
- **Exchange**

Traps x6:
- **Magic Cylinder**
- **Mirror Force**
- **Spellbinding Circle**
- **Time Seal**
- **Waboku**
- **Dust Tornado**

How to Build a Rex Raptor Dinosaur Deck

By: Jason Cohen (Lord Tranorix)

You all know who Rex Raptor is, don't you? He's the **Dinosaur duelist**, whose specialty is pounding his opponents with his powerful monsters. Okay, we've never actually seen him win a duel, but that doesn't make him any less awesome. Here's how to build a good Rex Raptor Deck.

Let's start with the big guy of the Deck: Serpent Night Dragon. Serpent Night is one of my favorite cards, and it's Rex's best card (after he loses his Red Eyes to Joey, that is). It's not very powerful, but we'll leave it in the Deck to give it a Rex Raptor feel.

The other big hitter is Black Tyranno. If the only cards your opponent has are monsters in Defense Position, Tyranno can attack directly!

More Great Dinosaur Cards:

- **Dark Driceratops** - A very powerful Dinosaur.

- **Gilasaurus** - You can summon him quickly.

- **Gagagigo** – A very powerful reptile

- **Element Saurus** – He weakens monster effects if you have Earth monsters in the field.

- **Mad Sword** - Like a mini-Dark Driceratops.

Other Great Cards for this deck:

- **Book of Moon** - Flip your opponent's monsters into DEF, very useful in this Deck. (see page 14)

- **Nobleman of Crossout** - Kills face-down monsters – works well with Book of Moon. (see page 10)

- **Ultra Evolution Pill** - Sacrifice a Reptile to summon a Dinosaur. It's great for getting out Black Tyranno.

- **Axe of Despair** and **United We Stand** are cards that make your monsters stronger.

- **Threatening Roar** - A Trap that stops your opponent from attacking; the mighty roar of the Dinosaurs scares him away!

This is a good place to start if you want to build a Rex Raptor Deck. It may not win all the tournaments, but it's sure to smash your friends!

1x Serpent Night Dragon
1x Black Tyranno
2x Dark Driceratops
3x Gilasaurus
3x Gagagigo
2x Element Saurus
2x Mad Sword Beast
1x Cyber Jar
1x Tribe-Infecting Virus
1x Breaker the Magical Warrior
1x Sangan
1x Sinister Serpent
1x Pot of Greed
1x Graceful Charity
1x Premature Burial
1x Snatch Steal
1x Heavy Storm
1x Mystical Space Typhoon
2x Book of Moon
2x Nobleman of Crossout
2x Ultra Evolution Pill
2x Axe of Despair
1x United We Stand
3x Threatening Roar
1x Ring of Destruction
1x Call of the Haunted
1x Mirror Force

10 Tips for Collecting and Trading Yu-Gi-Oh! Cards!

By: Joseph Lee

Yu-Gi-Oh! is a trading card game, so it's not surprising that trading is needed for building collections and decks. Here are some good guidelines whether or not you are trying to build the strongest deck or coolest collection!

1. Above all else, make friends, be nice, and **have fun!** Aside from the obvious, it makes trading easier.

2. Keep your cards in **sleeves or binders** with pages made for trading cards. Cards for collections should go there right away. Sleeves make cards last longer and they may still be good enough for a collection after use.

3. Only trade when you can **pay attention** to trading. Don't trade while dueling! You risk getting cheated in both places!

4. People make fake cards. Some even try to sell them as the real deal. Easiest way to avoid being tricked is to **only** trade and buy from people you know and **trust.**

5. Price guides are useful, but **don't** just go by card name, as many cards are reprinted. Vampire Lord is available in four rarities; Common, Ultra Rare, Secret Rare, and 1st Edition Secret Rare!

6. The better a card is for playing, the **more** it is worth. Sometimes Super Rares are worth more than Ultra Rares because of this fact!

7. **Don't be fooled** by a card being shiny. The easier a card is to get, the less it is worth. Starter decks come with their own Ultra Rares!

8. Keep your collection **organized** in a simple manner. Putting cards in order of your favorites isn't helpful for someone else, but going by name or set numbers is easy to follow.

9. If you can afford it, buy a whole box at once! It should be cheaper than buying the same amount of packs one at a time, so long as the store sells by the box. It also makes it more likely you'll get rare cards.

10. Go to **tournaments** just to trade. Players trying to fix up their decks at the last minute will trade you above value for a card they need.

The Rarest Cards

By: Bill "Pojo" Gill

It's always fun to guess at which are the **rarest** and most **collectible cards.** Here are a few cards that you probably won't see in your lifetime. All are easily worth several thousand dollars. If I had to guess … I'd estimate that all the Blue Eyes Ultimate Dragon cards would fetch about **$20,000 each** at auction.

T3·01 Blue Eyes Ultimate Dragon

This card was given to the 2001 Asian Champion as First Prize. **Only one** is known to exist.

T3·02 Summoned Skull

This card was given out at the 2001 Asia Championship as the 2nd Prize. **Only one** is known to exist.

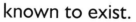

T3·03 Angry Kuriboh

This card was given out at the 2001 Asian Championship as the 3rd Place Prize. **Only one** is known to exist.

T3·04 Gemini Elves

This card was given out at the 2001 Asian Championship as the 4th Place Prize. **Only one** is known to exist.

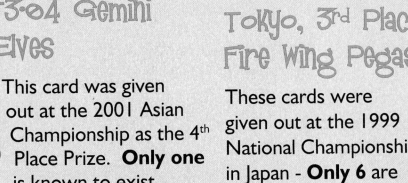

T3·05 Red Eyes Black Dragon

This card was given out at the Asian Championship as the 5th Place Prize. **Only one** is known to exist.

Tokyo·1st Place Blue Eyes Ultimate Dragon

These cards were given out at the 1999 National Championship in Japan – **Only 2** are known to exist.

Tokyo, 2nd Place Meteor Black Dragon

These cards were given out at the 1999 National Championship in Japan - **Only 4** are know to exist.

Tokyo, 3rd Place Fire Wing Pegasus

These cards were given out at the 1999 National Championship in Japan - **Only 6** are known to exist.

WCS·EN401 Ulevo

These cards were given as the 2004 World Championship Prizes - **Only 2** are known to exist.

WCS·EN402 Meteo the Matchless

These cards were presented as 2004 World Championship Prizes - **Only 6** are known to exist.

Which is more Powerful?

By: Ken Hartwick

A lot of duelists think Blue-Eye's White Dragon is the strongest monster. There are also duelists who think Dark Magician is the strongest. Dark Magician can combo with other cards. But if you look at the decks that win tournaments, you never see Blue-Eye's White Dragon or Dark Magician. Why is that?

Instead, tournament winners play monsters like **Sangan, Spirit Reaper, Exiled Force** and **Magician of Faith.**

Why is it that a monster like Magician of Faith that has an attack of only 300 is played in winning tournament decks and not Blue-Eye's White Dragon which has an attack of 3000?

It's because Magician of Faith has a **great effect!** It can get a used magic card out of your graveyard and back into your hand so you can use it AGAIN! This is great for cards like Swords of Revealing Light, because you are only allowed to have one Swords of Revealing Light in your entire deck. Your opponent is not going to like losing another 3 turns of attacks for a second time.

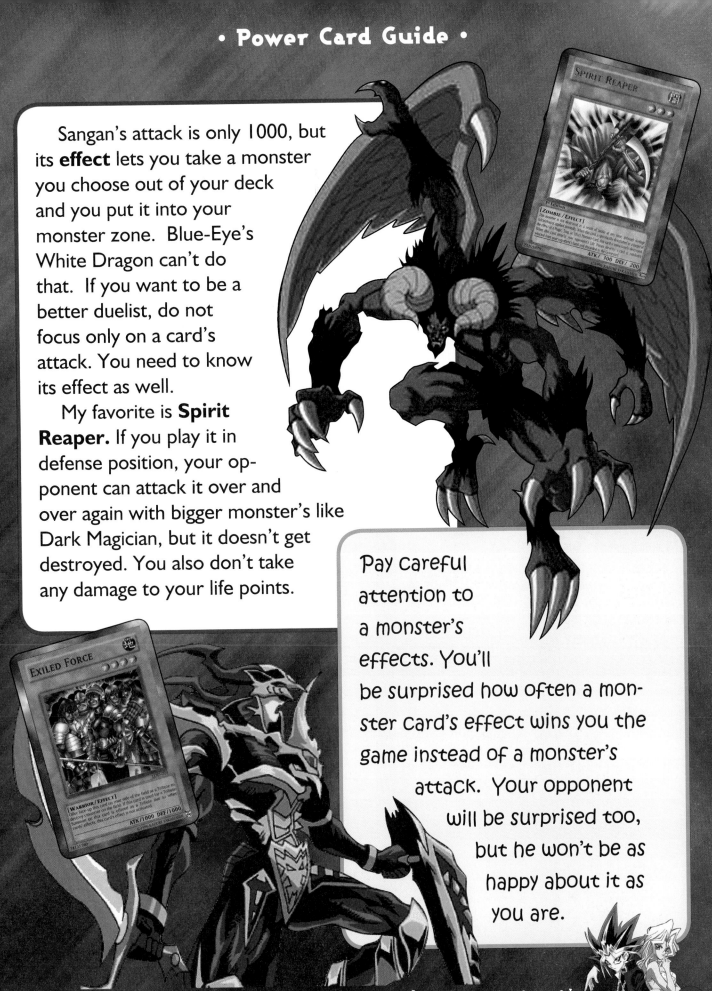

Sangan's attack is only 1000, but its **effect** lets you take a monster you choose out of your deck and you put it into your monster zone. Blue-Eye's White Dragon can't do that. If you want to be a better duelist, do not focus only on a card's attack. You need to know its effect as well.

My favorite is **Spirit Reaper.** If you play it in defense position, your opponent can attack it over and over again with bigger monster's like Dark Magician, but it doesn't get destroyed. You also don't take any damage to your life points.

Pay careful attention to a monster's effects. You'll be surprised how often a monster card's effect wins you the game instead of a monster's attack. Your opponent will be surprised too, but he won't be as happy about it as you are.

Which Card is Better: Dark Magician or Blue Eyes White Dragon?

By: SHECKii

Have you guys wondered which card is better? Is it the **Dark Magician** that Yugi plays? Or is it the **Blue Eyes White Dragon** that Kaiba plays?

Let's have a look!

The main way to bring out a Dark Magician is through a card called Skilled Dark Magician. Skilled Dark Magician is a 1900 ATK/1700 DEF Level 4 monster. 1900 ATK?! He's bigger than 7 Colored Fish and La Jinn the Mystical Genie of the Lamp! He'll knockout almost all of your opponent's Level 4 or lower monsters. He's a great creature huh? All you need to do is

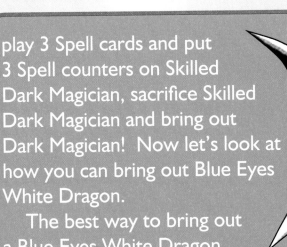

play 3 Spell cards and put 3 Spell counters on Skilled Dark Magician, sacrifice Skilled Dark Magician and bring out Dark Magician! Now let's look at how you can bring out Blue Eyes White Dragon.

The best way to bring out a Blue Eyes White Dragon is using the card Kaibaman. He's a 200 ATK/700 DEF Level 3 monster. He's not as good as the Skilled Dark Magician, but look at its effect. Tribute Kaibaman to special summon Blue Eyes White Dragon from your hand! That's amazing right? If you have these two cards, your opponent has to go against Blue Eyes White Dragon in the first turn! Also, you can use the card Reinforcement of the Army to bring out Kaibaman from your deck to your hand!

I personally like the Skilled Dark Magician/ Dark Magician combo better. But you should **play-test** both combos and see which one you like better.

Point of Note:

- Kaibaman can't special summon Blue Eyes from the deck.
- Skilled Dark Magician can special summon Dark Magician from the deck and the graveyard.
- You can special summon Blue Eyes White Dragon with other Dragon monsters as well, with Lord D plus Flute of the Summon Dragon.

Pojo's Guide to Yu-Gi-Oh! ★Leagues!

By: Michael Lucas (EMOD)

Yu-Gi-Oh! leagues can be scary to new duelists. For most, this will be the first time they see more than 20 players competing at the same time. There are a few things new players should do to make sure they have a good time. Here are the most important rules:

Upper Deck's Yu-Gi-Oh! Leagues and Official Tournaments give you the opportunity to obtain cards you can't get anywhere else. Photo courtesy of Upper Deck.

Know the basics

While stores may run their leagues differently, a few things are **almost always true:** You **don't** have to bet cards on duels – usually you're not allowed to bet at all. Most places allow trading only if the League Leader is there and okays the trade. Stores often have their league sessions 1 day a week (usually Saturday or Sunday morning), for 2 hours. If you don't know the store's rules, **ask!**

Know what your cards are worth

The last thing you want to do at a league is trade, then find out a week later you gave up a $40 card for a $2 card. Ask other older players before you make a trade, or invest in a price guide.

Know what you're looking for

If you want certain cards to add to your deck, make up a list of them so you remember what to ask for when trading.

Keep an eye on your possessions

If your parents are with you, have them hold your trading binder. If not, don't let it out of your sight. This way, it won't get lost or stolen.

Know the card game rules

It's a good idea to print out the card rulings and bring them with you; this way if someone tries to play a card wrong, you can show them why it's not allowed, or, if someone plays a card you've never seen before, you can make sure you don't accidently break a rule.

MOST OF ALL, HAVE FUN! YOU'RE THERE TO MEET PEOPLE, DUEL, AND TRADE, SO MAKE THE MOST OF IT!

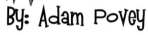

Top Ten Dragon-Type Monsters

By: Adam Povey

Since Yu-Gi-Oh! was created, **Dragon monsters** have been the biggest, baddest monsters in the game. They have huge ATK's. These are some of the most dangerous monsters you can play.

10. Paladin of the White Dragon

(SKE-024): As he is a Ritual Monster, you need time to play him. His 1900 ATK will always do damage. He also brings out Blue-Eyes White Dragon for free.

9. Blue-Eyes White Dragon

(SKE-001): The original Dragon, this is the best monster for two tributes. All the cards that bring it out for no tributes just make it better.

8. Kaiser Glider

(DCR-051): People should play this card more often. 2400 ATK that can pretend to be 2500 is good. Getting rid of a card when it's destroyed is great!

7. Tyrant Dragon

(LOD-034): A famous Dragon, but not wonderful. He can attack twice and do lots of damage with his huge ATK. However, he can be expensive to play and buy.

• Dragon Card Guide •

6. Troop Dragon

(LOD-042): Most Dragons need tributes. This card gives you tributes. Your opponent attacks it and you can get another one. You can then tribute it for a big Dragon to punish your opponent.

5. Spear Dragon

(LOD-035): This doesn't need a tribute. It can do damage when your opponent defends, hitting your opponent when he thought he was safe. Dragons don't normally behave this way!

4. Twin-Headed Behemoth

(SD1-004): Another card that helps you get out bigger Dragons faster. It defends you, then comes back to give you a tribute for a better Dragon.

3. Masked Dragon

(SD1-009): When this card is destroyed, you get another Dragon when you need it. It protects your Life Points, gets you tribute monsters, and lets you get what you want from your Deck!

2. Horus the Black Flame Dragon LV8

(SOD-008): When you play this Dragon, half of your opponent's Deck is useless. Only the best players can get around this master of the game.

1. Chaos Emperor Dragon

(IOC-000): When you play this card, people can hear the boom for miles. It has 3000 ATK. It can explode and win you the game. It is the most dangerous and one the most valuable cards in the game!

A Look Into the Future

By: Justin Webb (a.k.a. DM7FGD)

Let's take a look at some very cool cards that are only in **Japanese** right now. Nobody knows when or if they will come out in English.

These cards are fun, but they're not worth using in your deck. They're cool to have though since they're the only cards in the game that actually show **anime** characters.

Pojo's UNOFFICIAL Yu-Gi-Oh! 2006 Trainer's Guide

Dark King Dragon Vandorgaron

Dark/Dragon - Level 8 - 2800/2500

This is a very cool-looking and powerful Monster Card. Its effect is activated when you use a Counter Trap Card, such as Magic Jammer, Seven Tools of the Bandit, or Divine Wrath, to stop an opponent's card. It lets you Special Summon Vandorgaron from your hand, and activate an effect based on what type of card you stopped. If you stop a Spell Card with a Counter Trap, you can deal 1500 damage to your opponent. If you stop a Trap Card, you get to destroy one of your opponent's cards, and if you stop a Monster Effect, you can choose a Monster in your Graveyard and Special Summon it.

Pharaoh's Judgment

Normal Trap

Effect: In order to use this card pay half of your life points to select one of the following effects. If you have a {Yu-Jyo} in your Graveyard, your opponent can't Set, Normal Summon, Special Summon, or Flip Summon any Monsters during this turn. If you have a {Unity} in your Graveyard, then until the end of the turn, it will stop the effects of your opponent's Spell/Trap cards on the Field, and they cannot activate or set any Spell or Trap cards.

Unity

Quick-Play Spell

Effect: This card lets you select one of your Monsters on the Field. Until the end of the turn, the chosen Monster's DEF strength becomes the total of the base DEF strengths of all of your face-up Monsters on the Field combined.

Yu-Jyo (Friendship)

Normal Spell

Effect: If you play this card, you must offer your opponent a handshake. If he accepts, both players' life points become equal (add both players' life points together, then divide by two). If you have a {Unity} in Hand, show it to your opponent, and he must accept your handshake offer.

Yu-Gi-Oh! Character Guide

By: Bill Gill

Yugi Moto

Yugi Moto is a freshman in high school. He lives with his grandfather, Solomon, above his grandfather's game shop. Solomon gave Yugi **the Millennium Puzzle** thinking Yugi would never solve it. But Yugi did complete the Millennium Puzzle and awoke the spirit of an Ancient Egyptian Pharaoh - **"Yami"**. The spirit of this Ancient Egyptian Pharaoh now lives inside Yugi, and they share each other's thoughts.

Yugi's Millennium Puzzle is one of seven Millennium items that exist in the world. Each Millennium item gives it's user a unique power. Yu-Gi-Oh! translates from Japanese to mean the **"King of Games"**. When Yugi

merges with Yami, he transforms into the invincible Game King.

Yami and Yugi are able to speak to each other with their minds. Yami has lost his memories. Yugi and his friends are on a quest to help Yami regain those memories, and defeat the bad guys that exist in the present and in Yami's forgotten past. Yugi & his friends have worked together to defeat the likes of **Pegasus, Bakura, Marik, Dartz** and many other villains.

Joey Wheeler

Joey Wheeler is Yugi's best friend. Joey is also a freshman at Yugi's high school. He has become a very skilled duelist. Joey has defeated many other great duelists including Rex Raptor, Bandit Keith, Bonz, Espa Roba, and Miko Tsunami. He has not yet beaten Seto Kaiba, and that has hurt his pride.

Joey has a sister named Serenity. Joey dueled in the Duelist Kingdom Tournament to earn money to pay for Serenity's eye surgery. Yugi won the tournament and gave Joey his prize winnings so Serenity could have her eye surgery.

Tea Gardner

Tea Gardner is a freshman at Yugi's high school. She dreams of going to New York to study dance. Tea is good friends with Yugi and Joey. She has a crush on Yami Yugi, and does all she can to support Yami and Yugi in their quests to defeat evil.

Tristan Taylor

Tristan Taylor is a freshman in high school. Tristan is great friends with Joey, but he is also very good friends with Yugi and Tea. Tristan doesn't duel very often, but he supports Yugi and Joey on their quests. Tristan has a crush on Serenity Wheeler, but hasn't told Joey yet.

Mai Valentine

Mai loves to play the Duel Monsters card game. At first, she cheated to win. She would scent her cards with different perfumes so she knew where they were in her deck. During the Duelist Kingdom Tournament, she lost all her star chips to Panik. Yugi won them back for her. After his act of kindness, she became Yugi's friend.

She has a crush on Joey, and Joey has a crush on her. After losing during the Battle City tournament, she joined with Dartz and his thugs to get better at Duel Monsters.

Seto Kaiba

Seto Kaiba is rich. He has his own corporation. He is driven in limos, travels in helicopters, and even flies around in his own Duel

Monsters Jet. Seto loves dueling, and is very cocky. He thinks he is the best duelist in the world. He knows that Yugi is good too, but won't admit it. He wants to beat Yugi so he can be known as the best Duelist in the World. Seto has beaten Yugi once, but he had to cheat to do it.

Ancient Egyptian artifacts indicate that Seto was a Priest during the time when Yami was Pharaoh. Seto refuses to believe that the mysteries of ancient Egypt and the Millenium Items predict his future.

Maximillion Pegasus

Pegasus is the owner of the Millennium Eye, another Egyptian artifact. The Millennium Eye allows him to read people's minds. This gives him a huge advantage in duels as he knows what cards people are holding, and what they plan to do.

Pegasus obtained the Millennium Eye during an archaeological dig and learned all the secrets of the ancient Duel Monsters game. He used this knowledge to create the Duel Monsters cards of the present. The most powerful cards he created were the 3 Egyptian God cards.

Pegasus started the first tournament seen in the cartoon: the Duelist Kingdom Tournament. His goal was to obtain all seven of the Millennium Items, starting with Yugi's. Luckily, Yugi defeated Pegasus in the finals of Duelist Kingdom.

Ryo Bakura

Bakura is a freshman at Yugi's high school. Bakura is the holder of the Millennium Ring. Much like Yugi's Millennium item, the Millennium Ring contains a Spirit — except Bakura's spirit is evil. People call Bakura's evil side Yami Bakura. Yami Bakura would like to obtain all 7 Millennium items, since he believes they will make him a god.

The powers of the Millennium Ring are unknown. It acts like a Millennium item detector, letting Bakura know where Millennium items are. Yami Bakura has stolen Pegasus's Millennium Eye and is hoping to get his hands on more Millennium items. He desperately wants to defeat the Pharaoh, Yami Yugi.

Marik Ishtar

Marik is the keeper of the Millennium Rod. The rod gives Marik the psychic ability to control someone else's body from a remote location. In other words, he can use people as his puppets. Marik is possessed by an evil spirit. The evil side of Marik wants to defeat the Pharaoh.

Marik believed he could become a god by obtaining and controlling the 3 Egyptian God Cards. The Egyptian God cards were the ultimate prizes of the Battle City Tournament. The finals of Battle City came down to Yugi versus Dark Marik. Yugi was able to destroy Marik's dark spirit and banish it from Marik's body. Yugi became the owner of all 3 Egyptian God cards.

Ishizu Ishtar

Ishizu is Marik's older sister. She also owns one of the Millennium items: the Millennium Necklace. Luckily, Ishizu does not have an evil side. The Millennium Necklace gives her the power to predict the future.

Ishizu predicts what happens in every round in the Battle City Tournament, but in her battle versus Kaiba, she is wrong. Kaiba proves he can control his own destiny when he defeats her by using his Blue Eyes White Dragon card and not his Egyptian God Card like she had predicted.

Shadi

Shadi is the protector of the Millennium items. He actually holds two Millennium items: The Millennium Key and the Millennium Scales.

The Millennium Key allows him look into one's heart and mind and see one's true self. Shadi understands that Yami Yugi is the true Pharaoh and he decides to leave Yugi alone for the time being. Shadi's origins and his goals have not been revealed in the cartoon. He plays a much larger role in the comic books.

Odion

Odion was adopted by Marik's and Ishtar's parents as a baby. Odion vowed to protect Marik from harm. He stands besides Marik on his quest to defeat Yugi, even though Odion does not believe in Marik's cause.

Bandit Keith

Bandit Keith is another skilled duelist. He is one of the bad guys in the Duelist Kingdom storyline. Bandit Keith and Joey don't get along. Bandit Keith cheated to get to the semi-finals of the Duelist Kingdom Tournament, but Joey beat him there. Bandit Keith uses a lot of machine monsters in his dueling deck.

Weevil Underwood

Weevil is a popular and skilled duelist who uses an Insect deck. He defeated Rex Raptor in a TV event. During the boat trip to the Duelist Kingdom tournament, he took all 5 of Yugi's Exodia cards and threw them in the sea. Yugi defeated him during the Duelist Kingdom Tournament anyway.

Rex Raptor

Rex is a very good duelist. He is known for his use of Reptile and Dragon cards in his deck. He is a thorn in the sides of Yugi and Joey, but he hasn't yet been able to defeat the good guys.

Duke Devlin

Duke is the Creator of Dungeon Dice Monsters (DDM). Duke challenged Yugi to a match of DDM, and Yugi won the match. Duke became one of Yugi's better friends after the match, and he helped Yugi at Battle City. He also went along on the trip to America when Yugi battled Dartz. Duke has a crush on Serenity.

Gozaburo Kaiba

Gozaburo is the founder of KaibaCorp and a famous chess player. Seto Kaiba challenged Gozaburo to a chess match. Seto bet Gozaburo that if he beat him, Gozaburo would have to adopt Seto and Mokuba from their Adoption Center. Seto won and Gozaburo adopted them. Gozaburo made Seto into a tough businessman so he could take over KaibaCorp. Seto did take over KaibaCorp and abandoned his adopted father.

Noah Kaiba

Noah is Gozaburo's son. When he was young, Noah was badly injured in a car accident. Gozaburo created a Virtual World for his son to live in as a normal child. However, Noah wished to have a real body and tried to trick Yugi and Kaiba into giving him their bodies. He was eventually defeated by Yugi.

Dartz

Dartz was the king of Atlantis 10,000 years ago. He fell under the spell of the mysterious Orichalcos and became evil. Dartz tried to obtain souls to help revive the Orichalcos God. Dartz eventually revived the God, but was defeated by Yugi and the Legendary Dragons.

Rafael

Rafael was on a cruise ship that got lost at sea when he was a young boy. He was stranded on an island with nothing but his Duel Monsters cards. He became good friends with his cards, and protected his creatures. Rafael was rescued by Dartz and became one of Dartz's servants. With Rafael's help, Dartz defeats Yugi in a duel and captures Yugi's soul to help revive the Orichalcos God.

Alister

Alister is also one of Dartz's servants. He is a pretty tough guy. Alister's brother was killed in a war. After he learns that KaibaCorp made the weapons that killed his brother, he wants revenge on KaibaCorp. Alister battles Seto in two duels. Their first match is a draw. Later, Alister hijacks Seto Kaiba's jet and challenges Kaiba to a duel on his jet. Kaiba defeated Alister.

Valon

Valon is an orphan. Dartz rescues him from prison after Valon was accused of setting fire to a church. Valon becomes one of Dartz's servants. Valon is fond of Mai and is jealous of Joey's and Mai's relationship. Valon has a great Armor deck but looses to Joey in a duel.

Summon Your Word Skills for Cartoon Cross Word!

Test your **true** Yu-Gi-Oh! cartoon knowledge. Use the clues below to fill in the puzzle on the next page. Some of the answers are only a character's first name, while others are a character's first and last name. How well do you know your Yu-Gi-Oh! characters? (Answers on the last page of the book).

ACROSS

4 Holder of the Millennium Necklace

5 Was King of Atlantis

6 Gets turned into a monkey while dueling Nezbit

7 Owner of the Millennium Ring

9 Loves Dinosaur Decks

12 Kid who was sealed in a Card by Pegasus

13 Gave Yugi the Millennium Puzzle

16 Accused Yugi of stealing her grandfather's Blue Eyes White Dragon card

17 Hijacks Kaiba's Plane and challenges Kaiba to duel

21 Perfumed her cards to win duels

23 Created Dungeon Dice Monsters

24 Holder of the Millennium Rod

25 Owner of the Millennium Eye

DOWN

1 Completed the Millennium Puzzle

2 Was Stranded on an island as a kid

3 Adopted Seto and Mokuba

8 Vows to protect Marik from harm

10 Beats Johnny Steps in a Dance Game

11 Has strong feelings for Mai

14 Threw Yugi's Exodia cards into the sea

15 Holder of the Millennium Key and Scales

18 Organizer of the Battle City Tournament

19 Wears a U.S. Flag bandanna

20 Group of bad guys formed by Marik

22 Needed an eye operation

Pojo's UNOFFICIAL Yu-Gi-Oh! 2006 Trainer's Guide

Summon Your Mightiest Knowledge to Beat ME!!!

Pojo? Puzzler?

Yu-Gi-Oh!
Character Word Search

Are you wise like Dark sage?

Find these character's names hidden in the puzzle on the right hand side.

ESPA ROBA

GOZABURO KAIBA

ISHIZU

JOEY WHEELER

MAI VALENTINE

MAKO TSUNAMI

MARIK

MOKUBA

NOAH KAIBA

ODION

PANIK

PARADOX BROTHERS

PEGASUS

RAFAEL

RARE HUNTERS

REBECCA HAWKINS

REX RAPTOR

SERENITY

SETO KAIBA

SHADI

SOLOMON MOTO

TEA GARDNER

TRISTAN TAYLOR

VALON

WEEVIL

YAMI YUGI

YUGI MOTO

ALISTER

ARKANA

BAKURA

BANDIT KEITH

BONZ

DARTZ

DUKE DEVLIN

Pojo's UNOFFICIAL Yu-Gi-Oh! 2006 Trainer's Guide

• Puzzle Page •

```
R Y K H K P H Q N O L A V Z R G H X R N
K N A F B W M T C H X U F I N B W R O O
A L I S T E R U Z I H S I L A O I U L A
S A S W V L J G E E Y M B N U R B T Y H
K N S R E H T O R B X O D A R A P C A K
P A I H E Z C V E M J I T X K I G E T A
Z K J K O T E I O Y T M N Y A U A C N I
O R I X W B N K X K W I L N V F R A A B
M A E I L A U U E M L H E E S C B A T A
A R B D M B H I H V O L E U A I Z D S X
K E Y O A I T A E E Y D S E A F A M I D
O N T Q R H W D C U R A I K L R A A R M
T D I D X A E N G C G A O O T E D R T R
S R N Z R K P I R E E R R Z N E R R B I
U A E O U Q M S P E U B I G U Y I M A Y
N G R D Y O I J E B X S E T O K A I B A
A A E N T D L L A L D R R R P A N I K W
M E S O A B X Z M A I V A L E N T I N E
I T U H J Z O L Q Z C I K P Q N L M H E
L A S J M G J D P G A G D H T B W A L V
D K J O T O M N O M O L O S K O Y R D I
Y R O J O H R K M L M I Y Q J O R I Y L
Y X W K P E Q P V G F T A Y Q A V K X R
M B T X Q E T G B Q I R C M C R Y Q Q J
H L Z L X I G Z P U E U G M T H C C Q M
```

Video Game Reviews

By Bill "Pojo" Gill

Game Boy Color

- Yu-Gi-Oh! Dark Duel Stories – 1 star – This game is lame. It's time for a Game Boy Advance!

Playstation 1

- Yu-Gi-Oh! Forbidden Memories – 2 stars – If you don't have a PS2, this game isn't too bad.

Game Boy Advance

- Yu-Gi-Oh! The Eternal Duelist – 3.5 stars – A better than average dueling game.

- Yu-Gi-Oh! Dungeon Dice Monsters – 3 stars – If you liked the match between Duke Devlin & Yugi, you may like this game.

- Yu-Gi-Oh! Worldwide Edition, Stairway to the Destined Duel – 5 stars – Most people believe this is the best Yu-Gi-Oh! game ever made.

- Yu-Gi-Oh! The Sacred Cards – 3 stars – This is a Role Playing Game type dueling adventure.

- Yu-Gi-Oh! World Championship Tournament 2004 – 4 stars – This is a very solid game!

- Yu-Gi-Oh! Reshef of Destruction – 3 stars – This is fun, but it takes a while to get cards that make a decent deck.

- Yu-Gi-Oh! 7 Trials of Glory – 3.5 stars – This is the newest Yugioh game. It's another solid GBA game.

Playstation 2

- Yu-Gi-Oh! The Duelists of the Roses – 3.5 stars – A pretty solid PS2 game.

GameCube

- Yu-Gi-Oh! The False-bound Kingdom – 1 star – GameCube owners should be crying. This game stinks. It plays like Monster Rancher.

Xbox

- Yu-Gi-Oh! The Dawn of Destiny – 4 stars – A fantastic game with good graphics and 1,000 cards.

Personal Computer (PC)

- Yu-Gi-Oh! Power of Chaos, Yugi the Destiny – 4 stars – A very cool game. Yugi's sayings get repetitive though.

- Yu-Gi-Oh! Power of Chaos, Joey the Passion – 4 stars – See above.

- Yu-Gi-Oh! Power of Chaos, Kaiba the Revenge – 4 stars – It's just like the other PC games. You can share cards between all 3 PC games, which is cool.

Pojo's Puzzler Answers